THE
HOLOCAUST
AND
BEYOND

FROM THE BOY WHO ESCAPED THE NAZIS

WOLFGANG HELLPAP

The Holocaust and Beyond: From the Boy Who Escaped the Nazis

Copyright © 2024 Wolfgang Hellpap. All rights reserved. No part of this book may be reproduced or retransmitted in any form or by any means without the written permission of the publisher.

Published by Wheatmark®
2030 East Speedway Boulevard, Suite 106
Tucson, Arizona 85719 USA
www.wheatmark.com

ISBN: 979-8-88747-199-0 (paperback)
ISBN: 979-8-88747-200-3 (ebook)
LCCN: 2024905513

Bulk ordering discounts are available through Wheatmark, Inc. For more information, email orders@wheatmark.com or call 1-888-934-0888.

For the children of Auerbach Waisenhaus, who were executed by SS soldiers, their lives brutally taken before they could grow up and become members of society.

For my mother, Klara Hellpap, who struggled to maintain the dignity of a mother to her child by courageously standing up to the Nazis and never abandoning her son.

CONTENTS

ACKNOWLEDGMENTS

Special thanks to my wife, Vilma Hellpap, for her loving encouragement to write this book, and to my granddaughter, Jasmine Hellpap, for her tremendous help in writing it. My warm appreciation to Warren Salinger, a fellow Holocaust survivor and friend, who transcribed my notes. And thanks to my editor, Jean Hennelly Keith, for her help in bringing my story to life.

Wolfgang Hellpap
Tucson, Arizona
Feb. 7, 2024

PREFACE

This is the story of my childhood and youth in Berlin, Germany, where I and so many others suffered gruesome experiences because of a cruel and evil man. In the aftermath of World War I, Adolph Hitler was appointed Chancellor of Germany, and from 1933 to 1945, he dominated that country and, increasingly, much of the rest of Europe. His ideology, as expressed in his book, *Mein Kampf,* was to create a superior race and eradicate those he considered to be of a subpar race, the Jewish people.

I am grateful to have survived the terrible things I had to endure and for the people who befriended me along the way. My memories are a constant reminder of the evil that racial hatred can inflict.

Wolfgang Hellpap

1

NIGHT OF BROKEN GLASS

One morning in 1937, when I was a young six-year-old German boy who thought he was also a Christian, I was a student in the second grade in Berlin's public schools in the section of the city of my birth, known as Wilmersdorf. By the end of that day, my teacher, Fraulein (Miss) Schwimmer, had shouted out my name, Wolfgang Hellpap, because it was on a list that she had been handed identifying me as Jewish.

The Nuremberg Laws, especially the first one, the "Law for the Protection of German Blood and Honor," decreed that Jews in Germany no longer could be considered German citizens and could no longer interact with Germans of more "pure" Aryan blood, who now were to be considered the "real" German citizens. The second of the Nuremberg Laws, the "Law of the Reich Citizen" stated that only those of German or related blood could become citizens of Germany. These laws were passed by the Nazi Legislature in September 1935, not in Berlin but in Nuremberg because that was where the Nazi Party was meeting. The laws were Adolph Hitler's first major achievement since having been appointed (not elected)German Chancellor by President Paul Von Hindenburg, on January 30, 1933, less than two years after my birth.

To make sure the Nuremberg Laws could be as perfectly written as possible, Hitler had appointed a team of a dozen high-ranking Nazi party members, all men, and sent them overseas to study other nations' racist laws. The first country they visited was the United States of America, home of the Jim Crow laws that enforced racial segregation in the southern United States beginning in the late 1800s, and the Chinese Exclusion Act passed by the US Congress in 1882.

My father's name was Max Hirchel. He was born in Berlin after his parents emigrated to Germany from Kraków, Poland. He married young and fought in World War I as a German. After the war, he eventually became a successful business owner of a large textile warehouse and a thriving retail store in Berlin that specialized in janitorial supplies. He was also a partner to another factory in Poland. When he met my mother, he was living in a luxury apartment in Berlin with his Jewish wife and two sons. My mother, Klara Hellpap (1902–1994), was hired to be his sons' nurse.

Klara was a pediatric nurse and a Christian Berliner. She and my father had a romantic affair, which resulted in her becoming pregnant with me. Although I was raised as a Christian, my father had me circumcised and registered with the Jewish Community Center in Berlin. He told my mother that he planned to divorce his wife and marry her. As a small child, I remember him visiting often, taking me and my mother on rides in his automobile. He was trying to build a father-son relationship with me. In addition to being a successful businessman, my father was also an amateur boxer. I remember meeting his friend Max Schmeling, the heavyweight champion of the world, and sitting on his lap. Although my father was successful and knew many notable people, he was not immune to Hitler's gestapo and was arrested several times. But Schmeling would always bond him out. In time, however, even Schmeling lacked the power to protect my father. My father eventually fled the country to live in China when I was still very young and I never saw him again. This was the fate of many German Jews who had contributed so much for Germany. The world would have been a much better place if Hitler would have never been born.

My religious affiliation was never an issue until the Gestapo made it so. My mother did whatever she could to keep me in school until a day in 1937 when my name appeared on my second-grade teacher's list as a Jew who needed to be expelled. From that moment on I stopped being a young Christian German boy and became a Jewish kid running for my life. The sounds that have stuck with me my whole life were not the teacher's nasty message expelling me from her class. They were those of my former classmates who spit on me and called me a "dirty Jew." When I ran away crying, they picked up rocks and threw them at me.

My mother tried hard to convince the Gestapo that I was not Jewish, even trying to prove to them that my circumcision, which had become the litmus test for denying Jewishness, had been medically necessary. They did not buy it.

She wanted to keep me with her where she lived on Zaeringerstrasse near the Kurfuerstendam in Berlin. The owner allowed this for a little while, but then he decided I had to leave. My mother asked her relatives to hide me, but they refused once the Gestapo insisted that I wear the yellow star of David that all Jews had been required to display. I also was ordered to report to the local precinct every two weeks. I was only six years old, and Finding a safe place for me to stay was our biggest problem.

When Kristallnacht occurred on November 9–10, 1938, the awful experience seared my memory. One window of our apartment faced out to the street, and it was through that window I was able to observe the carnage below. The streets were full of German Jew-haters screaming "Down with the Jews," waving flags with the Nazi swastika (hakenkreuz or "hooded cross") and shattering the store-front windows of Jewish-owned businesses, my father's among them, that resulted in shards of broken glass piling up in the street. Many of the rioters, driven by the words of Nazi propaganda minister Joseph Goebbels, carried the glass shards.

"Come in, Wolfgang!" my mother screamed. I was only seven at the time and was very scared and crying. I left my window perch when my mother told me to do so.

The air was heavy with dark, acrid smoke from the burning synagogue nearby. It was set ablaze by the rioters, as Jewish houses of worship were destroyed all over the country. No efforts were made to put them out due to accompanying orders from Nazi headquarters to let them burn. Smoke from burning synagogues in Berlin hung like a heavy towel over the city and added to the horror of that night. Very commonplace German folk morphed into thugs ready to loot the ruined stores and kill any Jew they encountered.

Adding insult to their injuries, Jewish store owners like my father were forced to pay for the damages caused by the rioters. My father's warehouse and store were destroyed.

In early 1939, I became ill with a very high fever and needed to go to the nearest hospital. But with anti-Jewish sentiment running at a high-fever pitch, no ambulance would take me. So, my mom and I took a streetcar to the Horst Wessel Hospital nearby. Though I had no proper paperwork, she was able to convince the authorities that I was a German, not a Jew. It was a very hardline Nazi facility where we were ordered to stand up every morning and scream "Heil Hitler," arms stretched in the appropriate Nazi salute.

As a result of Kristallnacht, my father took his Jewish family and moved to Shanghai, China, in 1939. He had done his best to be a part of my life in Berlin. When he came to say goodbye to me, I was still in Horst Wessel Hospital and so we met in the hospital's backyard, amidst hugs and the tears my seven-year-old self shed.

I never saw him again, but some years later, we were notified by the Jewish Community Center of Shanghai (which was dissolved by the Japanese occupiers of China in 1941) that he had died in China of meningitis at age fifty-four. I had no further contact with his Jewish family.

My mother and I had lived on Zaeringstrasse for about two months. After my father left and I was released from the hospital, we moved to a one-room apartment on Winsstrasse. It was leased by two older sisters who told me to stay in the room all day. Because I was no longer in school, I spent my time looking at books and newspapers while trying to learn how to read and write. When I did get out on occasion, I saw the Hitler-Jugend (Hitler Youth) wearing their shiny uniforms and had pangs of desire to wear them too.

Food in stores was rationed and Jews were given only the minimum to survive.

Wolfgang at about eighteen months,
winter of 1933, Berlin, Germany.

2

CAPTIVE AT AUERBACH

One day in when I was eight years old and staying with some relatives, I decided to go out and the police caught me. Because I was Jewish, they told my mother I would have to enter a Jewish orphanage in Berlin's Prenzlauer Berg district called Auerbach Waisenhaus. It was 1940 and the war was raging, with Hitler's army occupying eastern countries like Poland and Hungary. Auerbach housed some two hundred children, aged one to eighteen. The home had been established in 1888 for Jewish orphans and abandoned children. Now it had become a small concentration camp for Jewish children who had been apprehended or taken to be "re-educated" to serve the "Fatherland." The all-Jewish staff collaborated with the Nazis.

I was assigned to a bed in the dormitory, a large building with about 150 beds and no closets or shelves. There were two and a half bathrooms which were almost always occupied. We all were required to be deloused, which meant being sprayed with a hose, after which we reported to the headmaster, Mr. Abramowitz, who gave us our marching orders.

We were instructed to learn how to "appreciate" the German Reich. I became good friends with another inmate of the orphanage, playing hide-and-seek, using bathrooms when available as hiding places, just to get away from the Jewish caretakers and Mr. Abramowitz. Lunch consisted of one slice of bread with lard and half a banana or pear. Afterwards we would play Schlagball, sort of like baseball, in the backyard. We were always watched by security or the Jewish teachers. We were allowed to play like that once a week.

At other times we had different assignments, like lessons on how to interact with other children and how to obey the teachers. I was immediately pegged as a potential violent boy and my teacher took pleasure in showing me the whip that he carried around with him. We were awakened every day around 6 a.m. to try and wash ourselves and dress. We had what they called night pots by our beds and it was our responsibility to wash them. All the rooms had loudspeakers in them. We were marched to the mess hall. Food was always an issue because we had very little of it. Breakfast was usually a small bowl of oatmeal and one slice of bread, a glass of water, and sometimes sour milk. After breakfast, the older children were led into classrooms, not to learn the basics of reading, writing, and arithmetic, but to be indoctrinated with

Nazi propaganda. We were also instructed on how the Nazi army functioned and about Hitler's goal of creating an Aryan race for Germany. Hitler had written about these plans and his hatred of Jews in his book *Mein Kampf* (My Struggle) while in prison in the 1920s. He described what was needed to get a pure German race, including restricting Jewish professionals like dentists, doctors, and lawyers, from having patients outside the Jewish race.

Auerbach was an awful place and became worse once the Germans started transporting some of the children to other camps. The Gestapo would come at night, usually between eight and ten, with a list of names, and the teacher, Mr. Abramowitz, really liked that. He had a whip, and whenever the Gestapo called out a name, he would crack that whip right at the child in bed, sometimes on beds, sometimes on heads. Imagine being eight or nine years old, hoping they would not call your name! When names on lists were called, the children whose names were called had to stand up and were then marched out and never seen again. Each night that passed without my name being on a list resulted in a morning of thanks that I was still around.

Kristallnacht changed everything for the worse. Auerbach Waisenhaus was an awful place and things there deteriorated quickly, to the point that I could find little joy or comfort in daily activities. Even the Jewish teachers became more vicious, especially Abramowitz. I began to feel that the best I could do at my own young age was to spend time with those even younger, like Arnold, age two, and Ruth, age three. We threw pillows in pillow fights and spun dreidels, though I never knew where they actually came from, since the Jewish teachers never seemed to prepare anything. Though in fairness to them, they probably had nothing with which to prepare.

The Gestapo were harsher and started coming around almost every night with their lists. When the Jewish festival of lights, Chanukah, approached, and I asked teacher Gorowitz, second in command to Abramowitz, if we could light a menorah. He almost hit me just for asking. Teachers were becoming more frightened of the Gestapo, fearing that their names might also appear on a list and that they, too, would be sent away.

Food was becoming scarcer. There still was a meager breakfast, but no lunch.

On September 1, 1939, Germany had invaded Poland and World War II began with early German *Blitzkrieg* wins, but also more difficult times for the Nazi army, leading to a greater urgency to destroy the Jewish race.

My mother could only visit me on certain days when visits were allowed. When she was able to come for visits, she brought me newspapers, some money, and we would talk.

I remember having this very strong feeling of wanting to leave, but it was impossible to escape because of the Jewish caretakers and the SS guards stationed outside the orphanage. Meanwhile, the nightly pickups by the Gestapo continued so that, by now, we had fewer than one hundred youngsters left.

One morning after breakfast, I went to babysit my two-year-old friend, Emanuel. I liked playing with him and tried to teach him some words in German and sometimes even in English. I don't really remember his country of birth. I shared some of my memories with him, about reading the Karl May books in which he described the wild west in the United States, its Indians, and their drums. I actually found a drum in one of the storerooms and pounded it for him until a Jewish teacher discovered us and took the drum away. My punishment was several days in solitary confinement.

When I was released from solitary, one of the Jewish teachers noticed me while he was talking with a Gestapo officer and ordered me to show him my hands. Then he whipped me three times on my palms, which caused the officer to laugh. I was sent me to a special room for confinement until the evening meal. The pain from the welts in my hands was excruciating.

By now I was eleven years old and very scared of the Gestapo's daily lists. I began to pray, asking God to help my mother get me out of there. I was very skinny—like all the other children because we were fed so poorly. We lost more kids almost every night, especially the older ones, whom the Nazis used for slave labor.

*The front and back of the Nazi ID for Wolfgang in 1941
when he was about ten years old and living in Berlin.*

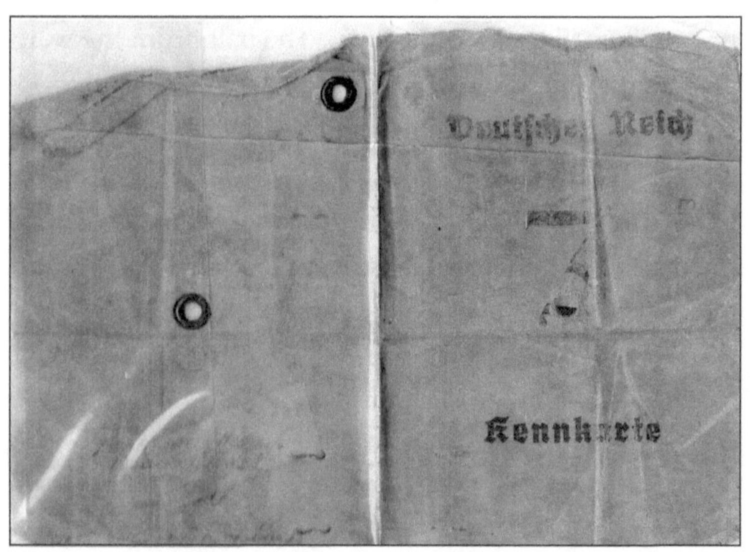

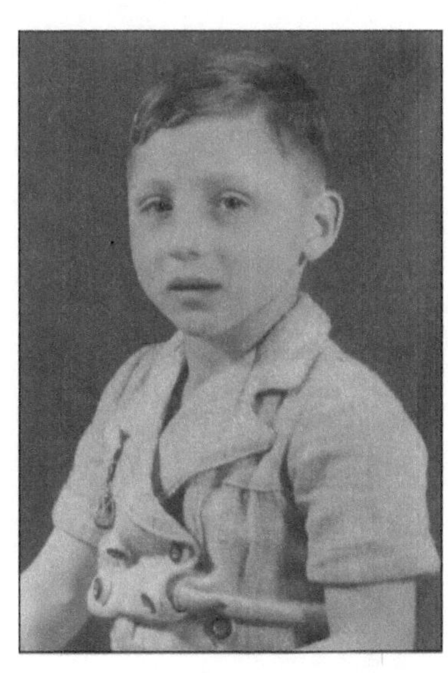

Wolfgang in 1941, assigned by the Nazis to live at Auerbach'sches Waisenhaus, a Jewish orphanage.

The last remnant of the wall at Auerbach orphanage with the names of the children who were murdered there by SS soldiers.

3

MASSACRE AND ESCAPE

A day I remember vividly came in November, 1942. We were awakened early in the morning and heard the engines of many trucks running in front of the orphanage. Abramowitz chased us into the dining hall, and I saw the SS men running up the stairs, three of them carrying rifles, their boots making a lot of noise.

I was in a group of ten kids, aged ten to fourteen, near the baby and small child section on the first floor, near the big entrance hall downstairs. The babies were in cribs or small beds, about fifty or sixty of them, right in the middle of the room. The SS soldiers were now facing us, with pistols and rifles drawn. They were just standing there as though they were waiting for someone. I moved far back to where the bathrooms were. An officer came up the stairs and by now the little ones started crying and screaming, seeing the SS soldiers in their boots, pushing the kids around. After an order was given by the SS officer, the soldiers began shooting the kids in the cribs. I immediately thought of Emanuel, my friend, who had to be in one of them. Blood was splashing everywhere as the other, more mobile kids, began running toward the rear of the room, many of them killed by shots to their backs.

At this point, many of the older teenage kids came running down the stairs. SS soldiers tried to hold them back. According to the records, the original volley of shots killed between ten and fifteen children. Many more would be murdered in the woods near Riga.

With the youngest children now dead, the SS troops were sent upstairs to round up the older youngsters. Shouted orders sent the rest of us to the waiting trucks on the street. Along with other boys, I ran toward the front as the soldiers stopped shooting and just pushed us ahead.

In the upper rooms of the orphanage, I later learned that the soldiers told the older boys to attack Abramowitz and the teachers. The soldiers had fun watching the shoving which caused the building to shake. Then we heard that the soldiers had killed Abramowitz and the teachers. By this time, the older boys were so scared by all the shoving and killing that they would not cooperate with the Nazis the way Abramovitz and the teachers had.

Now the SS started to herd us toward the trucks on the street and I got pushed and thrown into one of them. One of the trucks carried the little corpses. We had heard of people being killed right in the trucks and other stories indicating the trucks would take us to a woods where the killings would take place. There were far fewer of us now, but all the kids who remained, including me, were very scared. There were two trucks for the living and one for the dead. All sped away, bruising us as we were thrown about.

When the trucks stopped, we were ordered out as the SS used their rifle butts to hasten our exit. I noticed that we were at the Grosse Hamburger Strasse in a huge plaza holding about one thousand people, most shouting or screaming as some were marched toward railroad tracks. We were now the last group facing the street, shivering because it was cold and most of us were wearing only pants and a shirt. I had a sweater too, which made me one of the lucky ones. The entire scene, with all the screaming and shouting, was very chaotic.

Suddenly, I noticed a little wall about twenty meters to the left pointing directly to the street. It was about five feet high, easy to climb, so I suggested to two boys near me that we try to escape over it. The soldiers were busy with the others, so we just sort of pushed ourselves toward the wall and climbed right over. I remember seeing one soldier there, but he did not shoot. I think I owe him my life. The trains were headed to a concentration camp in Riga. Many kids went to concentration camps and most of them died there.

Our immediate problem was that we had yellow stars on our clothing, some even sewn onto the shirts we wore. We were now on a very public street and needed to get away as quickly as possible. The neighborhood was quiet and fairly deserted. I knew where I was because the Prenzlauer Allee was not far from there and I also knew that it had been bombed. I figured once I reached the Allee, I could hide in one of those bombed-out buildings and figure out what to do next. The other two boys, who lived in a different direction from me, tried to get home to their parents, but I never found out what happened to them. We were all about eleven years old.

I did not to try to reach my mother because I was afraid the Gestapo might already know about my escape. So, I decided to try to make it to my Uncle Max's home, which was a house on a pretty big spread of land in Zehlendorf, a Berlin borough at that time. I had to walk mostly in the evening hours, always alert for police. Dusk was the best time to travel on foot because in November it was still light with less people about. I found food in garbage cans and even ate dog food left out for pets. When I had entered Auerbach orphanage, my mother had given me some money, which I had been able to conceal in my pants from the authorities. I was now able to use that to phone my mother and arrange to meet up with her at certain points along the way. She agreed with my plan to reach Uncle Max, but neither she nor I wanted to be seen together. My yellow Jewish star was still a problem, but I was afraid to be spotted removing it.

Once in Lichtenfeld I saw some boys in Hitler Youth uniforms following me, so I stopped and waited for them, telling them that I was not feeling well and was on my way home from school. A strong "Heil Hitler" convinced them I was legitimate. My Jewish star must have been hidden by my sweater. That experience did, however, show me how dangerous the streets were, so I planned to travel the rest of the way to Zehlendorf by bus. The buses were double-decker, and I always went to the top because there were usually few or no people at all up there.

It took me three weeks to reach my uncle's house. I was very hungry and dead tired. Finally arriving, I went through the large front gate and knocked on the front door, which my Aunt Adina opened.

"Oh boy, Wolfgang, your mother told us you were on your way. Come on in and I will fix you something to eat."

Her words alone warmed me, and I thought I was in heaven just at the thought of sitting down for a real meal.

She told me that Uncle Max and her two daughters, Addi and Senta, would be home soon and that they all knew of my arrival, though at that time, both girls were members of the Hitler Youth, in German, known as the BDM, Bund Deutsche Maedchen (Organization of German Girls).

My uncle arrived first and told me right away how welcome I was in his house. I felt happy that people in my family, besides my mother, treated me normally. Pretty soon both girls came in and said they were happy to see me. Senta was a little shy but my uncle explained to them that I was their cousin and had nowhere else to go. He told them they had to be quiet about my being there and that their cooperation was needed. And they agreed!

When we sat down together to eat, it was a real treat for me after scrounging for food while on the run. My

Uncle Max explained to me that I had better keep out of sight of the neighbors during the day, fearing that they might include some Gestapo officers. Later in the afternoon it might be safer, though he encouraged me to be very careful. I would spend most of my days inside, trying to be helpful to the family in some way.

On weekends, I helped my uncle with yard work, like cutting or trimming trees, mowing the lawn, etc. My mother came to visit and always brought something with her to eat or to read. Soon the Allies started bombing day and night, and as a result, the falling bombs became more consistent and Zehlendorf became a target. After staying there for six months, I was hiding in a favorite water hole when a bomb fell within twenty yards of me. Alarmed, my older cousin ran toward the big hole the bomb had made but I was not hurt.

Unfortunately, word spread among the neighbors about a boy who was almost hit by a bomb, and my mother decided I had better leave before the authorities came to investigate

.

4

ON THE RUN AGAIN

My mother and I continued to look everywhere for safe places for me to live, most of the time staying with family, but they would let me stay only a few nights at a time before I had to hide elsewhere. I lived mostly on the streets, hiding in old sheds, bombed-out buildings, or anyplace I could find. I was so young and thought that there must be something awfully wrong with me. Of course, I was afraid of the police and would try to hide my star of David so I could "pass" as a non-Jew. When I was on the streets, my mother met me as soon as she could to bring me food and money and to tell me where to meet her next. We had to be very careful.

My mother had some friends near Weissensee, not far from the Jewish cemetery, who said they were willing to take me. The husband, Paul Kampf, was once a member of the Communist party. He had two sons, Rudi and Kurt, who, like Senta and Addi at Uncle Max's, had no problem with my being there. So, in mid-to-late 1943, my mother took me to them on public transportation.

Their apartment was on the top floor, which made it seem safe for me to move freely. Paul worked as a janitor and his wife, Berta, stayed at home with the boys. Rudi was thirteen and Kurt was twelve. Although a little older than me, they befriended me. Sometimes I went out with them without wearing my star, doing things like ice skating and even going to the movies.

Of course, during the week on school days, they went to their classes while I stayed home, hiding in the attic, which had a bed, a table, and a chair. In those days, women had a weekly wash day, and my mother was always came there for that. So, wash day became a day to which I looked forward to because I could be with my mother the whole day.

The boys had to belong to the Hitler Youth, and though they knew me to be Jewish, just like my cousins in Zehlendorf, they never gave me away. I felt good because I did not have to be on the streets, homeless and hungry. Because Jews were not allowed to go into the bunkers (air raid shelters) or basements, during bombings, I had to stay upstairs.

I stayed with the Kampf family for about six months. One time during the bombings, a fire started in the lower part of the house while I was upstairs in the attic. We were scared that it would spread through the entire house, and I prayed that we would be spared and safe. Luckily, we were.

After the bombing and fire my mother decided she and I should be together, whatever might come our way. So, we moved in with my other uncle, Uncle Hans, who welcomed us warmly. Not so his wife, who was quite mean to us, always feeling we were a burden to them which, of course, we were. Food was in short supply and Lotte, Hans' wife, understandably, wanted to feed her family first.

I always felt that Lotte hated me. She often pushed me around and called me "the little Jew." My mother confronted her over this, but she never changed. In the mornings, I had to ask for permission to use the bathroom. Breakfast was a hassle and always left me with a feeling of being terribly unwanted in Lotte and Hans' home.

I often spoke to my mother about this, but since it was now 1944 and the German war effort was stalled in defeats and retreats, she told me not to worry too much; the war would soon be over.

I stayed in our room as much as I could, studying, reading, and writing. I was also interested in learning English, but I only had one book in English and an English travel brochure that my mother had once given me, which made it hard.

My mother was now working as a telephone operator in Berlin's center and would sometimes come home telling us that she had overheard some Nazi official talking about the cattle car transports to the camps. They talked quite freely about the treatment the poor souls squeezed into these cattle cars received. There were no windows, air came in only through cracks in the doors, and there was no food.

By now, the bombing had become so bad that Berlin was almost entirely destroyed. The many dead people in the streets and the ruins of the destroyed houses made that very clear. Because I was a Jew, I could not use the air raid shelters that had been built to protect people. So, I stayed mostly in our room, praying that our building would be spared. I saw many neighborhood buildings that were hit, people crying and dying.

The Gestapo was still arresting Jewish people and sending them to concentration camps. In fact, there were deportations to the camps all through 1944. The Nazis seemed to be hurrying with their destruction of the Jewish race before they lost the war.

The constant bombing of Berlin—my hometown and Germany's capital city—certainly convinced most of its inhabitants that they were going to lose the war, even though Reich Marshal Hermann Goering, second-in-command to Hitler, had promised them better days and that Berlin would be spared the bombing. But the American bombings during the day combined with the British and Russian planes at night proved Goering wrong.

At work, my mother overheard other conversations between Nazi officials who were talking about the continuing deportations of Berlin's Jews, what was the best way of killing them, since shooting did not seem to be quick enough. The Wannsee Conference of January 1942 had come up with the idea of gassing them, and the Auschwitz-Birkenau concentration camp became the best and most efficient place where that was done.

My mother had also become aware of the fact that the Gestapo had developed a lot of information about Paul Kampf and maybe even of my living with the Kampf family. She was now staying with her brother, Hanz Hellpap, on Kesselstrasse, in Berlin center, and she suggested I come back to live with her. It was now mid-1944 and I was 13 years old. The constant bombing was scaring people all over Berlin. Many houses were bombed out; many people were killed. Food was extremely scarce and there was very little to eat. Meanwhile the Nazi army was being defeated in Russia by the Soviets and in Western Europe by the Americans and the British. Despite this, the Nazi propaganda machine continued to say that the Germans were winning, even as the Russians entered Berlin!

Bombing became so constant and deadly that daily life grew almost impossible. Still, Hitler's minister of propaganda, Joseph Goebbels, promised the German people that Germany was in possession of a deadly bomb that would secure victory for the Germans.

My mother and I never believed this, since we knew that Russian troops were advancing in and around Berlin, district by district. Even going to the grocery store by Kesselstrasse required passing a tower where a Russian sniper had found a spot at the top from which he would shoot and kill Germans on the street.

The members of the Kampf family who hid Wolfgang from the Gestapo. Paul Kampf at far right, circa 1943.

5

FREEDOM

One day in early May 1945, my mom and I were in a cellar of a home on Kesselstrasse when, through a window, we spotted a Russian tank coming down the street. My uncle sent me out wearing my yellow star to greet the tank. A Russian lieutenant on top of the tank noticed me and jumped down to hug me, then screamed that Hitler was dead. As I was crying for joy, he entered his tank and came back with some Russian food for us. I tore the yellow star off my shirt, hugged my mother and we both cried for joy that the nightmare was over. It was May 8, 1945.

The Russian soldiers were given two days to celebrate their victory. Berlin was in ruins by now, no food, no supplies, and we heard about the property damage and rapes perpetrated by Russian soldiers.

We were eating horse meat and you had to stand in line to buy that. My mother found a job in a Russian kitchen, which enabled her to bring lots of food home.

I was now fourteen and a free kid again!

It had been six and a half years since Kristallnacht on November 9, 1938. For six and a half years I had lived in constant fear of being discovered, wearing my yellow star, always hiding. Sometimes I stayed with the families of my mother, her brothers and their wives, their kids, who were Hitler Youth and BDM (Bund Deutsche Maedchen) members, sworn to honor the Fatherland, and salute the Fuehrer, arms stretched out and high. Yet, in all that time, while sometimes calling me "the little Jew," they never gave me away. It had been six and a half years since I witnessed the horror of Kristallnacht, hugged my father for the last time—six and a half years of never knowing if I would see another sunrise.

Yes, I was free again. No more fear of being chased or arrested. It took another day or so, after welcoming the Russian tank and its lieutenant, for the Nazis to stop broadcasting their propaganda and telling Germans that the invading armies would soon be expelled because Germany was about to have a weapon (an atomic bomb) that would win the war. Fortunately, of course, that never happened.

And now, though Martin Luther King Jr. had not yet given his "I Have a Dream" speech at the Lincoln Memorial, if he had, I would have echoed his words: "Free at last. Free at last. Thank God almighty, we are free at last."

Berlin, however, wasn't free. It was a divided city, now consisting of four parts that were really like four separate municipalities. The Americans, English, and French occupied the western parts of the city, while the largest section was governed by the Russians. The Russians were given the largest part because they had fought the decisive battle that ended the war. Because Americans had a reputation for fairness, everyone wanted to be in the American sector, but we happened to live in the Russian portion. The way the geography worked out, the Russians also controlled most of the area surrounding the city, through which all food to feed Berlin's people had to come. In effect, the Russians controlled all incoming supplies.

We still lived in our uncle's house and food for us and his family became our main concern. One day, I decided to try to reach some farmland outside of the city. To get there, I had to take a very overcrowded train and find a spot on the roof over which a lot of people were fighting. Because I was a kid with a large backpack strapped tightly to my back, I was able to squeeze into an empty spot. It took about four to five hours to travel 100 miles to arrive in a little farm town, where I left the train. Then I walked about another ten miles to the nearest farm.

The farmer told me that if I worked for him for two weeks, I could fill my knapsack. I did that, then loaded my backpack with eggs, sausage, and bacon, all the food I liked. Next, I set out for the return trip to the train station, soon running into a Russian army truck filled with young soldiers. Seeing me, they quickly jumped off, took my knapsack filled with food, and slapped me around a bit. I was lucky to get away and now felt that I would have to return home empty-handed. But, while waiting for night to come, I found a potato field nearby and filled another bag with them. Then I boarded a train heading my way and found a spot on the roof, just as I had done before. My mother and uncle felt very sorry for me when I returned home and told them my story.

Soon I learned that my uncle and his wife had a son who was a soldier in the Wehrmacht (unified armed forces of Nazi Germany), who had been wounded in the fighting around Berlin. My cousin was in a rural hospital nearby, where I was able to visit him. I was still wearing one of my yellow stars, sewn onto a sweater, just to let German people know that I was one of Berlin's Jews whom they had tried to kill.

Finding enough food to feed the five of us—Uncle Hans, Aunt Late, an eight-year-old boy who lived with us, my mother, and me—was becoming such a struggle. Quite suddenly, my mother and I decided we no longer wanted to live in Germany. In order to find a way out, we had to get to the American sector, which was a real problem because the subways and buses were controlled by the V.P. (Deutsche Volkspolizei or German People's Police). Germans were not allowed to move from one sector to another, but we tried anyway, taking the U-Bahn subway to get to the West. Vopos, as the East German Volkspolizei were called, patrolled the trains, but since we had no luggage, they did not suspect us and let us through.

We made it to Orienburg, where a big refugee camp was located in the American sector. Jewish aid organizations, especially HIAS (Hebrew International Aid Society) looked for surviving families and children. HIAS decided that I should be transported to Palestine (visas to America were unavailable) with about twenty other Jewish boys from eleven to sixteen. I was fifteen at the time. My mother, though she was also classified as a refugee, could not come with me and was told she had to wait for one year before coming to Palestine. She was sent to Bergen-Belsen, a former concentration camp, now a refugee camp for people waiting to be shipped abroad. Saying goodbye to my mom was painful and brought many tears, though we did believe that we would see each other again in a year.

The other boys and I boarded a bus bound for Paris and stopped at a shelter with lots of beds to spend the night. I was talking with a boy my age named Gerhard, who also had spent the war years, like me, hiding in Berlin.

After two nights somewhere in Paris, we proceeded to a small town outside of Paris called Caille-sur-Eure. We were assigned to a beautiful and very large old house in the center of the town with a river flowing next to it. We played a lot of soccer and swam in the river, which was high with water and often pretty wild. Once it actually swept one of our boys away, but I was able to run toward the nearest bridge, from which I could grab him. He was blond with blue eyes. We called him our little Nazi!

We were there for about two weeks, getting to know each other, studying and learning a good bit of French. Then we were on the bus that took us to Marseille, a beautiful harbor city in southern France with a zoo almost like the one in San Diego. We were driven to a big mansion that looked a lot like Berlin's Auerbach Orphanage. There were already some French refugee kids there. We were assigned two to a room and I ended up in a room with Gerhard.

In Marseille, we waited for a ship to go to Palestine, at that time a country controlled by the British. But it was also the land where Theodor Herzl, considered the Zionist founder of Israel, dreamed about our promised land where we could return as Jews and be free from all pogroms and persecutions.

We were told that, once on board the ship, we were to hide Jewish young men because there were no visas being given to Jewish young men for Palestine.

We took field trips while in Marseille and had plenty of tasty food. It was like heaven—payment for all the hard times we had lived through, remembering that we were always just a few steps away from being caught by the Gestapo and death. In Marseilles people remembered the years of Nazi occupation and were eager to hear our stories. I enjoyed my time in Marseilles a great deal and always felt that it made up just a little bit for all the deprivations I experienced as a child growing up in Berlin, both before and during the Nazi times.

Now I could walk the streets as a free boy, have proper nutrition, and even listen to contemporary music.

Gerhard and I became good friends. He told me a lot about his experiences in Berlin. Like me, he had been thrown out of school. He became homeless after his father died, and his mother, who was Christian like mine, abandoned him. So as a child of nine, he was in constant danger of being captured by the Nazis. He stayed with various relatives of his mother and some friends of his father and then took to the streets like me. And like me, he was liberated by the Russians.

After getting up in the morning one day, our escort lady from HIAS came in and told us that the ship that would take us to Haifa had anchored in the harbor. It was a big ship, she said, and it would carry us together with a lot of other passengers to Palestine. Some of the passengers would leave the ship in Egypt. The escort also said that each of us should hide in our cabins. British spies were on board our vessel and were looking for young Jewish men and boys trying to enter Palestine to sabotage the British occupation troops there.

Gerhard and I shared the small cabin to which another young man also was assigned, and we were expected to hide him from the British. We were also expected to feed him and see to his safety.

I was seasick soon after sailing from Marseille, yet I tried to hide from the British spies. I always tried to save some of my breakfast and dinner to bring to our "guest." We spent some of our time trying to read from Hebrew books, trying to learn the language.

We had plenty to eat; the food on board was very good. We also had days with pretty bad Mediterranean storms. The ship anchored briefly in Alexandria, Egypt, to disembark some passengers bound for there, but we were not allowed to disembark. Haifa was just a day away! We arrived in Haifa by mid-January, 1946.

Our ship became known as a "youth ship," the first such vessel to arrive in Palestine after the end of World War II, and we were met with parties and other celebrations. The young Jewish men who had been hiding aboard the ship were arrested by British soldiers, who boarded when the ship first docked, then they were sent to a camp on Cyprus run by the British for detained Jewish men and youth. We were shipped to Tel Aviv.

Wolfgang (bottom row, center) was among the first youth group to reach Palestine after World War II; photo taken in Marseille, France, 1945.

6

A NEW LIFE IN A NEW LAND

Some other kids and I ended up in the Hannah Chichic Agricultural Camp, which was huge! We now had to go to school to catch up on our general education and to learn to read and speak Hebrew. I enjoyed my time here very much, coming so soon after my six and a half years of dread. I remember crying tears of happiness for just being there.

I began to acclimate myself more and more to life at Hannah Chichic. In the mornings, I went to school, mostly to study Hebrew and math, finding the mathematics much more troublesome than the language. By afternoon, I would work in the agricultural areas of the complex. I loved working with the horses and was proud of what I could do with them. By 1946 and 1947, we had plenty of those equine friends. They were used to pull wagons, and I loved driving the teams that pulled them, bringing supplies to the complex.

We worked from 7 a.m. to 5 p.m., but always started with a very large breakfast that consisted of eggs and potatoes and often even included some chicken. Tasks included digging potatoes from the ground, getting hay for the animals, and doing various farm chores. There were frequent rest periods and plenty of in-between snacks. The exercise associated with the farm work made me feel really good, and the fresh air and great nourishment helped too. What a difference from the life at the orphanage, which I remembered all too well. We were learning to become adults in a new land, learning about the agriculture that sustained it and how to farm it.

I grew better and better at my studies, and I learned a lot of English from the British soldiers. I was now speaking four languages: German, Hebrew, French, and a bit of English. In general, however, we and the rest of the community considered the British to be oppressive occupiers. Even our Arab neighbors, with whom we got along very well, did not like them. I remember every morning, Arabs coming into our neighborhood to sell fresh fruit, and us often taking that fruit without paying for it, for which I am still genuinely sorry.

Because there were always clashes between us and the British soldiers, the English authorities imposed frequent curfews, demanding that everyone be off the streets by 8 p.m.

In 1947, through news reports and other sources, we learned that the bubonic plague had broken out in

Tel Aviv. The British, in trying to control this pandemic, were exceptionally brutal, stationing soldiers at important street corners and crossings, shooting at people who seemed to be wobbly, acting in many ways like the Germans during Nazi times, rough and insensitive. People were quarantined; houses were barricaded.

I was now sixteen years old, finished with school, and needing to decide what to do with my life. Gerhard, my good friend, had decided to go to a moshav, a cooperative community of individual farms, to study more about agriculture.

I was sent to Kibbutz Kvutzat Shiller to further my education. It was a community founded by German-Jewish settlers, where people worked well together, shared everything, and treated everyone equally.

I then learned that my mother, who had remained in Germany, had received a visa to come to Palestine. I welcomed her there, and we were offered a place to stay where we could live together at the kibbutz. I thought that because it was a German-Jewish kibbutz, she would be able to speak German there, but unfortunately, nobody wanted to talk to her in German—no one wanted to speak German anymore—and she did not know any Hebrew. Because it was so shortly after the end of World War II, and the memories of the Holocaust and what Germans had done to six million Jews were fresh, nobody wanted to speak or hear German.

The Kvutzat was a strict all-inclusive kibbutz, which

meant that everything was shared. For example, if our family got a TV, all families got a TV. There was a common kibbutz kitchen and a big building where everyone went for their meals.

Work was assigned. Some of us worked in agriculture, some in more mechanical areas like the motor pool, some in building new structures, some in nursing and day care for children. Those placements were made from week to week. My mother, a professional baby nurse in Germany, was given that kind of work. There was even a small hospital that had one doctor. Life, I recall, was very dull. Several times I was ordered to work in a vegetable field managed by a man later charged with selling some of the field's crop for private profit. He was charged with embezzlement and kicked out of the kibbutz.

There were also frequent visits by English authorities, inspecting the grounds, looking for people they called illegals. We did not treat these people well, making fun of them, never offering them refreshments of any kind, though the weather was always very hot.

After a few more months, my mother and I felt that life on the Kibbutz was not for us. She realized that she could probably find work in Tel Aviv as a baby nurse in private homes and make much more money doing that, and that I could learn a trade.

Soon the plague was under control, and we found a place to stay in an old mansion that had been owned by an Arab sheik. With the little money we had, we were only able to afford one room. All the rooms were rented separately, and bathrooms and showers were shared by all the tenants. Living conditions in the sheik's house were terrible. It was very old and very primitive and the room we lived in was filthy and infested with vermin.

Soon, I found a job as a refrigeration mechanic, while my mother found work as an infant nurse in a private home. We were now finding our way into the new Israeli society in Tel Aviv.

While a trainee in the refrigeration business, I took evening classes to learn more about my new trade. There, I became very good friends with another boy, Peter Bergman (he was called Moshe in Hebrew and I was called Zeev). He had been born in Vienna and was able to escape the Nazis with his father, traveling through France and Spain on their way to find a ship, a freighter that would take them to Palestine. Peter was learning how to become a watchmaker. We spent a lot of time together in Tel Aviv, going out, meeting girls.

I proceeded with my work as a refrigeration repairman, employed by an English company named Thompson and Thompson. I worked the day shift, installing new refrigeration equipment. My ability to convince my customers that they needed to install new power lines for their new equipment earned me extra money.

The British mandate to govern Palestine was coming to an end. The United Nation's Resolution 181, which called for the division of British-mandated Palestine into two states, one Jewish, one Arab, was passed on November 29, 1947. Peter and I followed the deliberations closely, listening to proceedings on the radio every chance we had.

As country by country was called to approve or not, we closely watched every response. We both had tears in our eyes as we realized that the resolution would pass and that the state of Israel would become a reality. Predictably, the Arabs did not accept the establishment of a Jewish state, while Jews embraced the news with great enthusiasm and celebration. I called my mother, who was working, and we both cried tears of joy on the phone.

My mom became an Israeli citizen, but the economics were not good and the new state's security was even worse. Half a dozen Arab countries were ready to attack. The Arabs, furious at having been evicted from (or somehow convinced to leave) their former homes, were now launching grenades into the streets of Tel Aviv.

On May 14, 1948, the State of Israel was officially declared by David Ben-Gurion, the Zionist leader who had long fought for a Jewish homeland for the Jewish people. He became Israel's founding prime minister and is considered the architect of the new Jewish state. (Prime Minister Ben-Gurion was in office from 1948 to 1954, and again from 1955 to 1963.) The next day, a group of Arab nations from Lebanon, Syria, Iraq, Egypt, Transjordan, and Saudi Arabia attacked the new Jewish state, deploying a military force under Egyptian command.

Klara Hellpap, Wolfgang's mother,
in Tel Aviv, December 1947.

From left, friend Peter Bergman, Klara, and Wolfgang, Tel Aviv, December 1947.

7

DEFENDING OUR HOMELAND

When the Arabs attacked, Peter and I knew that our new state was in real trouble, so we decided to join the Haganah. The Haganah was a Jewish paramilitary group formed in 1920 to defend the growing Jewish population in British-run Palestine against Arab attacks. It was one of several military factions in the new state.

Though I was only sixteen, I was accepted, and nineteen-year-old Peter and I were sent off to boot camp. There were some old British buildings in the camp, but it consisted mostly of tents. We were issued field uniforms soon after our arrival. I started my training by learning how to shoot with one of the old German rifles that were shipped to us from Czechoslovakia, now the Czech Republic. We were told to aim a few centimeters off-target, a little to the left, to hit the intended target. We were trained in all phases of attack and defense. Haganah was very badly equipped and to make it look like we had more cannons and tanks than we really did, we had to construct and install props that were look-alikes for the absent tanks and artillery.

One night, as Arab troops were spotted approaching our quarters, our officers sounded the alarm, shouting "They are storming across the field toward us, so grab your weapons and hit the trenches," which had been built at the end of our quarters. I grabbed my rifle and jumped into the nearest trench. Later, it became clear that the attacking Arabs were Iraqis, known as sloppy and poor soldiers. I was in my trench with another soldier and started shooting at anything that moved, no specific target in mind. I was very scared and came close to wetting my pants. We had fixed our bayonets, shooting while screaming at the same time. The Iraqis were also screaming, so it was quite chaotic, when suddenly, just as the enemy approached our trenches, a group of Palmach appeared. The Jewish Palmach was an elite force of the Haganah, with many more weapons, like grenades and machine guns, and quickly took over the battlefield. Some of us got into hand-to-hand fighting, but we were told to retreat as our enemy was driven back. Though we were just raw recruits, we proved ourselves in combat. The props that we had built to make us look stronger than we actually were worked!

Troops from different Arab countries had attacked, but we were fighting for our lives and our new country, and we all returned safely to our quarters where we were checked for injuries and then treated for them. I always thought the Arabs were fighting for their lives and country as well, a country they felt had been stolen from them. We believed that our cause, dating back to Theodor Herzl's founding of Zionism in 1897, to create a state of their own for the Jewish people, was stronger than theirs, strengthened by the unbelievable experience of the Holocaust.

We continued our training after our combat experience, but within three days were done and received our assignments. Our whole platoon was sent to a Haganah division already fighting the Transjordanian Frontier Force in Jerusalem.

These Transjordanian soldiers were trained by the British army and the British had given the Arabs the fortifications that they themselves had built. Peter and I were fighting them, but they overwhelmed our battalion, forcing us to retreat. We passed by an orthodox synagogue and tried to convince the congregation's members to flee, but they wanted to stay and pray. We literally had to drag them out.

Our battalion was split as we retreated and as Peter and I were running across a field, I was hit in the leg. I was bleeding badly but Peter was able to drag me to the nearest aid station.

We had suffered some heavy casualties and because of the many wounded there, it was chaotic. The doctors and nurses were overwhelmed, unable to treat everyone. Seeing that my wound was so close to the bone, the doctor wanted to amputate. Peter pointed his rifle at the doctor and said, "If you amputate, I will pull the trigger." The stunned doctor then just told the nurse to put me in the back of the station somewhere. The bullet had gone right through my leg, but the bleeding eventually stopped. I was on a stretcher for about four hours when, finally, my leg was bandaged and I got some medicine. I just had to wait to be transported to a hospital. Peter had to report back to the fighting. Eventually some others and I were put in an ambulance and taken to a military hospital in Tel Aviv. Upon arrival, we were triaged and taken to different wards.

Because my papers wrongly said I had lost my leg, I was taken to an orthopedic surgeon for further evaluation, where she discovered that, in fact, I had not lost that leg. But in the process, they discovered that I was underage, which led me down the road to being discharged. That took a while, so during that wait time, I was assigned non-combat duties. I was sent to Negev, where we were assigned the duty of watching Arab prisoners, who were mostly Egyptians. The Egyptian army had been ordered to capture Tel Aviv and, in that effort, had sustained heavy casualties.

One day, while watching the Egyptians, I overheard some of them talking in German, so I asked one, "Who are you?" He replied, "We are mercenaries from Germany, fighting the Jews." I immediately reported them to my officer, and they were quickly sent to a special camp.

When the Arabs discovered that they could not defeat us, a ceasefire was reached on May 2, 1948, leading to a lot of Palestinian Arabs leaving their homes, which were now in the new Jewish State of Israel, for resettlement in Arab countries. We lost a lot of land in old Jerusalem, but our newly established state survived the Arab onslaught.

Wolfgang (center) poses with several Haganah soldiers.

Newspaper clipping of Wolfgang, Haganah "Soldier of the Month," right after boot camp outside of Tel Aviv, 1948.

Israel Prime Minister David Ben-Gurion, celebrating the Seder together with Haganah soldiers, Jerusalem, 1948. Wolfgang, not pictured, was somewhere in the crowd.

*Wolfgang, Haganah soldier in
the Battle for Jerusalem, October 1949.*

8

LOOKING WEST

In 1949, I was discharged from the new Israeli army. I went back to Tel Aviv and to my old job as a refrigeration mechanic. Our working conditions were primitive and we had to rely on public transportation to take us to our jobs. I worked that job for about three years, and my mom and I still lived in the awful residence that the sheik had abandoned. We tried to get visas for the United States or Canada, but, at that time, it was impossible. We later heard that it would be much easier to obtain the U.S. visas.

With our living conditions in Israel being pretty bad, my mother and I decided to return to Germany. However, in 1953, the State of Israel did not allow Israeli citizens who were full Jews to emigrate to Germany. My mother, of course, was considered Aryan and did not have this problem. I would not be eligible to emigrate to Germany until I claimed my German citizenship. I was forced to do that in order to emigrate to the U.S., which was my real desire. That was the picture when I finally obtained an exit visa from Israel. I felt that I had done my duty for my father's sake for the establishment of the State of Israel.

That same year, 1953, my mother and I left on a ship bound for Italy, then took a train to Germany. We did not have much money, but we were confidant that I would find work back in Germany. We arrived in Naples and stayed there for one night, then we took a train to Munich, Germany, via Florence, Italy, where we had to change trains. By now, we had only fifty dollars between us, and we still had to spend one night in Munich, on our way to Stuttgart. We were headed there because my Aunt Martha, my mother's sister, owned a sanatorium in Bad Liebenzell in the Black Forest not far from Stuttgart.

When we arrived, Aunt Martha welcomed us, making us feel very thankful that we could stay there for a while. We stayed for a month, then went to Stuttgart to apply for visas for the U.S. We found a room in a pension, and I quickly found work.

I went to the Hebrew Immigrant Aid Society (HIAS) to apply for refugee visas to the United States for me and my mother. First, the Jewish Community Centre in Stuttgart had to make sure that I was a survivor of the Holocaust and that I was really Jewish. A rabbi took me to the bathroom to check my penis to see if I was really circumcised, which was ironic because during the Nazi times, my mother had tried to convince the Gestapo that my circumcision had been medically necessary, an argument she had lost. She had even provided a doctor's certificate, but the Nazis did not buy it because my circumcision had been documented in the records of the Jewish Community Center in Berlin, which the Nazis had checked.

HIAS agreed to sponsor me and fund my journey from Germany to the U.S., but my mother would have to pay her own way. We waited in Stuttgart for two years, until 1955.

9

AMERICA

As our Stuttgart waiting time began, I had to find work, so I went immediately to the employment office and found that they only had one opening which was for an elevator operator in a U.S. Army hospital. When I told the woman with whom I was talking that I was an elevator mechanic, even though I actually had no idea about elevator mechanics, I got the job.

I went to work and quickly learned that my supervisor was a Berlin native like me. When I told him that I really did not know too much about elevator mechanics, he just said, "Stick with me." Soon a call came in that an elevator was stuck, and I was the only mechanic available. My foreman was not available either, so I grabbed my tool bag and went to the roof where the motors were located. Desperate, I took a hammer in hand and gave one of the motors a good whack. And, presto! The motor started to run. Then I heard people shouting that the elevator had started to move, which proved that I was actually an elevator mechanic! However, that motor had to be replaced, and, it seemed, so did I. My Berlin foreman came to tell me I could no longer work there. However, he also told me of a refrigeration repair job opening up in Ludwigsburg, and since I now had experience in the field, I got that job, which consisted mostly of repairing refrigerators in homes. I also was given a car to drive so I could inspect refrigerators and other devices in the homes of dependents of U.S. troops to make sure that when appliances were given to the new arrivals, they would be in good operating condition. It was a great job because I was driving around in U.S. Army-licensed vehicles and the pay was very good. When we discovered appliances that needed work, we took them back to the shop for repair. To get to work in Ludwigsburg every morning, I took the train.

After two years of this, 1953–1955, my mother and I finally obtained our U.S. visas. By this time, my mother and I were pretty settled into our daily life in Germany. But our aim was always to establish our lives in the U.S. We received German passports with the U.S. visas stamped in them. Then HIAS took over, designing a complete plan for our trip, which we had to follow. They paid for my entire trip and for the costs associated with settling in the United States.

Our journey to the new world began with a trans-Atlantic ship crossing in the fall of 1955, beginning in the German port of Bremerhaven on a ship named the

USS *General W. C. Langfitt*, which carried many other refugees. We arrived in New York City and stayed there for two days before leaving for San Francisco, our destination, with a slight detour to Omaha, Nebraska, where I had been asked by a soldier named Gerson to pay a visit to a friend at a U.S. veterans home. My mother and I stayed in Omaha for about a week, which threw us slightly off schedule.

Although it was somewhat interesting to see parts of Omaha, with lots of factories and other signs of industry, overall, it left me fairly unimpressed. The next train ride took us to Oakland, across the bay from San Francisco. This was a mistake because the HIAS people expected us to arrive in San Francisco. By now, we were out of money, so we had to walk across the Oakland Bay Bridge, which is 8.4 miles long, to get to Sutter Street by way of Market Street in San Francisco. I had a Hohner harmonica, which I was able to sell along the way for $30.

We finally arrived at the HIAS door on Sutter Street and, luckily, there was still someone there who was able to take us to our new home on Van Ness Avenue, across the street from Tommy's Joint, a very famous San Francisco restaurant and bar. HIAS then found me a job and a used car and soon, after getting a California driver's license, I started working as a delivery driver, quickly getting to know the San Francisco area pretty well.

By May 1956, six months after our arrival in the US, I received a letter from the president of the United States, inviting me to become a member of the U.S. Army. I

claimed that very spotty knowledge of the English language should disqualify me from serving, but they said
"NO," that they would welcome me anyway, and so I ended up at Fort Ord in Monterey Bay, California, where I
did my basic training. We were all afraid that we would be
sent to Korea, where even though the war was officially
ended, many skirmishes were still going on.

Because of my fluency in the German language, I was
ordered to Germany, with stops for interrogation by the
CIA along the way because I had relatives living in East
Germany. Once they were satisfied, they sent me by train
to New York. There we boarded a ship that turned out to
be the same one that had brought me and my mom to
New York. We boarded about 3,000 troops as part of the
10th Armored Division. En route, a soldier died on board,
and because helicopters were unable to retrieve him, we
detoured to the nearest port, which was in Newfound-
land. When we landed, the local people were astounded
to see a ship with 3,000 American soldiers aboard. We
next proceeded to Bremen, Germany, but because we did
not have adequate provisions for what became a ten-day
journey, we weren't able to eat for the last two days. When
we arrived in Bremen, we got paid. The German vendors
realized this, and they sold everything at double the price.
They were surprised that I was able to speak with them in
German.

We were then shipped to our various stations. I served
the remainder of my two years in the army as an interpret-

er in post-World War II Germany, which was the front line of the Cold War in Europe for forty years.

While I had been living in Stuttgart waiting to emigrate to the United States, I met and married my first wife, Aurelia, in 1955. She did not get a visa with me at that time, but she did get one when I was drafted into the army. While I was traveling to Germany with the army, she was heading to America.

In 1958, when I returned to the United States and was discharged from the army, Aurelia and my mother picked me up in New York. We bought a car and traveled across the United States to San Francisco. I tried to get back into refrigeration work, but the union did not let me. I needed a job, and was hired by Soule Steel Company, an ironworks business. In 1959, my wife was pregnant, and our first son, Daniel, was born. We bought a house in San Francisco in 1962 and in 1964, our second son, Ronald, was born. I studied and became an industrial lab technician and worked for Soule for about twelve years, until 1972. Aurelia and I eventually divorced.

In 1978, I married my second wife, Vilma. She was from Honduras and a cook, and we operated a Mexican restaurant together in San Francisco until we moved away nearly twenty years later. We had a son, Michael, who died at only 36 years old after returning from the war in Afghanistan. He was the father of two children, Desiree and Xavier. After my mother died in 1996, Vilma and I relocated to Tucson, Arizona, where we still have our home. For years, we have been associated with a Holocaust Survivors group. The horrible things that I survived, especially as a child and youth, have become a constant reminder of what evil racial hatred can do.

Wolfgang, serving in the United States Army, 10th Armored Division, pictured here with a tank battalion, Germany, 1957.

Wolfgang and Vilma Hellpap, far right, gather with other members of the Jewish Family and Children's Services Holocaust Survivors Group. Photo taken in Sierra Vista, Arizona 2005.